The Gender of Sound

The Gender of Sound

ANNE CARSON

Published in 2025 by Spiral House, an imprint of Silver Press.

'The Gender of Sound' by Anne Carson was first published in
Glass, Irony and God, New Directions, 1992.
Reprinted by permission of New Directions.

ISBN-13: 978-1-7393717-9-1

Design by Rose Nordin
Typeset in Adobe Caslon Pro by Jay Drinkall
Printed and bound in the UK by CPI

EU GPSR Authorised Representative: Logos Europe, 9 rue Nicolas Poussin, 17000, La Rochelle, France.
contact@logoseurope.eu

3 5 7 9 10 8 6 4

It is in large part according to the sounds people make that we judge them sane or insane, male or female, good, evil, trustworthy, depressive, marriageable, moribund, likely or unlikely to make war on us, little better than animals, inspired by God. These judgements happen fast and can be brutal. Aristotle tells us that the high-pitched voice of the female is one evidence of her evil disposition, for creatures who are brave or just (like lions, bulls, roosters and the human male) have large deep voices.[1] If you hear a man talking in a gentle or high-pitched voice you know he is a *kinaidos* ('catamite').[2] The poet Aristophanes puts a comic turn on this cliché in his *Ekklesiazousai*: as the women of Athens are about to infiltrate the Athenian assembly and take over the political process, the feminist leader Praxagora reassures her fellow female activists that they have precisely the right kind of voices for this task. Because, as she says, 'You know that among the young men the ones who turn out to be terrific talkers are the ones who get fucked a lot.'[3]

This joke depends on a collapsing together of two different aspects of sound production, quality of voice and use of voice. We will find the ancients continually at pains to associate these two aspects under a general rubric of gender. High vocal pitch goes together with talkativeness to characterise a person who is deviant from or deficient in the masculine ideal of self-control. Women, catamites, eunuchs and androgynes fall into this category. Their sounds are bad to hear and make men uncomfortable. Just how uncomfortable may be measured by the lengths to which Aristotle is willing to go in accounting for the gender of sound physiognomically; he ends up ascribing the lower pitch of the male voice to the tension placed on a man's vocal chords by his testicles functioning as loom weights.[4] In Hellenistic and Roman times doctors recommended vocal exercises to cure all sorts of physical and psychological ailments in men, on the theory that the practice of declamation would relieve congestion in the head and correct the damage that men habitually do to themselves in daily life by using the voice for high-pitched sounds, loud shouting or aimless conversation. Here again we note a confusion of vocal quality and vocal use. This therapy was not on the whole recommended to women or eunuchs or androgynes, who were believed to have the wrong kind of flesh and the wrong alignment of pores for the production of low vocal pitches, no matter how hard they exercised. But for the masculine physique vocal practice was thought an effective way to restore body and mind by pulling the voice back down to appropriately manly pitches.[5] I have a friend who is a radio journalist and he assures me that these suppositions about voice quality are still with us. He is a man and he is gay. He spent the first several years of his career in radio fending off the attempts of producers to deepen, darken and depress his voice, which they described as 'having too much smile in it'. Very few women in public life do not worry that their voices are too high or too light or too shrill to command respect. Margaret Thatcher trained for years with a vocal coach to make her voice sound more like those of the other Honourable Members and still earned the nickname *Attila the Hen*.[6] This hen analogy goes back to the publicity surrounding Nancy Astor, first female member of the House of Commons in 1919, who was described by her colleague Sir Henry Channon as 'a queer combination of warmheartedness, originality and rudeness ... she rushes about like a decapitated hen ... intriguing and enjoying the smell of blood ... the mad witch.'[7] Madness and witchery as well as bestiality are conditions commonly associated with the use of the female voice in public, in ancient as well as modern contexts. Consider how many female celebrities of classical mythology, literature and cult make themselves objectionable by the way they use their voice. For example, there is the heartchilling groan of the Gorgon, whose name is derived from a Sanskrit word **garg* meaning 'a guttural animal howl that issues as a great wind from the back of the throat through a hugely distended mouth'.[8] There are the Furies whose high-pitched and horrendous voices are compared by Aiskhylos to howling dogs or sounds of people being tortured in hell (*Eumenides*).[9] There is the deadly voice of the Sirens and the dangerous ventriloquism of Helen (*Odyssey*)[10] and the incredible babbling of Kassandra (Aiskhylos, *Agamemnon*)[11] and the fearsome hullabaloo of Artemis as she charges through the woods (*Homeric Hymn to Aphrodite*).[12] There is the seductive discourse of Aphrodite which is so concrete an aspect of her power that she can wear it on her belt as a physical object or lend it to other women (*The Iliad*).[13] There is the old woman of Eleusinian legend, Iambe, who shrieks obscenities and throws her skirt up over her head to expose her genitalia.[14] There is the haunting garrulity of the nymph Echo (daughter of Iambe in Athenian legend) who is described by Sophokles as 'the girl with no door on her mouth' (*Philoktetes*).[15]

Putting a door on the female mouth has been an important project of patriarchal culture from antiquity to the present day. Its chief tactic is an ideological association of female sound with monstrosity, disorder and death. Consider this description by one of her biographers of the sound of Gertrude Stein: 'Gertrude was hearty. She used to roar with laughter, out loud. She had a laugh like a beefsteak. She loved beef.'[16]

These sentences, with their artful confusion of factual and metaphorical levels, carry with them as it seems to me a whiff of pure fear. It is a fear that projects Gertrude Stein across the boundary of woman and human and animal kind into monstrosity. The simile 'she had a laugh like a beefsteak', which identifies Gertrude Stein with cattle, is followed at once by the statement 'she loved beef', indicating that Gertrude Stein ate cattle. Creatures who eat their own kind are regularly called cannibals and regarded as abnormal. Gertrude Stein's other abnormal attributes, notably her large physical size and lesbianism, were emphasised persistently by critics, biographers and journalists who did not know what to make of her prose. The marginalisation of her personality was a way to deflect her writing from literary centrality. If she is fat, funny-looking and sexually deviant she must be a marginal talent, is the assumption.

One of the literary patriarchs who feared Gertrude Stein most was Ernest Hemingway. And it is interesting to hear him tell the story of how he came to end his friendship with Gertrude Stein because he could not tolerate the sound of her voice. The story takes place in Paris. Hemingway tells it from the point of view of a disenchanted expatriate just realising that he cannot after all make a life for himself amid the alien culture where he is stranded. One spring day in 1924 Hemingway comes to call on Gertrude Stein and is admitted by the maid:

> The maidservant opened the door before I rang and told me to come in and wait. Miss Stein would be down at any moment. It was before noon but the maidservant poured me a glass of *eau-de-vie*, put it in my hand and winked happily. The colourless liquid felt good on my tongue and it was still in my mouth when

> I heard someone speaking to Miss Stein as I had never heard one person speak to another; never, anywhere, ever. Then Miss Stein's voice came pleading and begging, saying, 'Don't, pussy. Don't. Don't, please don't. Please don't, pussy.'
>
> I swallowed the drink and put the glass down on the table and started for the door. The maidservant shook her finger at me and whispered, 'Don't go. She'll be right down.'
>
> 'I have to go,' I said and tried not to hear any more as I left but it was still going on and the only way I could not hear it was to be gone. It was bad to hear and the answers were worse . . .
>
> That was the way it finished for me, stupidly enough. She got to look like a Roman emperor and that was fine if you liked your women to look like Roman emperors . . . In the end everyone or not quite everyone made friends again in order not to be stuffy or righteous. But I could never make friends again truly, neither in my heart nor in my head. When you cannot make friends any more in your head is the worst. But it was more complicated than that.[17]

Indeed it is more complicated than that. As we shall see if we keep Ernest Hemingway and Gertrude Stein in mind while we consider another vignette about a man confronting the female voice. This one is from the seventh century BC. It is a lyric fragment of the archaic poet Alkaios of Lesbos. Like Ernest Hemingway, Alkaios was an expatriate writer. He had been expelled from his home city of Mytilene for political insurgency and his poem is a lonely and demoralised lament from exile. Like Hemingway, Alkaios epitomises his feelings of alienation in the image of himself as a man stranded in an anteroom of high culture and subjected to a disturbing din of women's voices from the room next door:

> . . . wretched I
> exist with wilderness as my lot
> longing to hear the sound of the Assembly
> being called, O Agesilaidas,
> and the Council.
> What my father and the father of my father
> grew old enjoying—
> among these citizens who wrong one another—
> from this I am outcast
>
> an exile on the furthest fringes of things, like Onomaklees
> here all alone I have set up my house
> in the wolfthickets . . .
>
> . . . I dwell keeping my feet outside of evils
>
> where the Lesbian women in their contests for beauty
> come and go with trailing robes
> and all around reverberates
> an otherworldly echo of women's awful yearly shrieking
> (*ololygas*).

ἀγνοις . . σβιότοις . . ις ὀ τάλαις ἔγω
ζώω μοῖραν ἔχων ἀγροϊωτίκαν
ἰμέρρων ἀγορας ἄκουσαι
καρυ[ζο]μένας ὦ (᾽Α)γεσιλαΐδα

καὶ β[ό]λλας· τὰ πάτηρ καὶ πάτερος πάτηρ
κα ⟨γ⟩γ[ε]γήρασ᾽ ἔχοντες πεδὰ τωνδέων
τὼν [ἀ]λλαλοκάκων πολίταν
ἔγ[ω . ἀ]πὺ τούτων ἀπελήλαμαι

φεύγων ἐσχατίαισ᾽, ὡς δ᾽ ᾽Ονυμακλέης
ἔνθα[δ᾽] οἶος ἐοίκησα λυκαιμίαις
. [ ]ον [π]όλεμον· στάσιν γὰρ
πρὸς κρ . [. . . .] . οὐκ † ἄμεινον † ὀννέλην·

.] . [. . .] . [. .] . μακάρων ἐς τέμ[ε]νος θέων
ἐοι[. . . . .] με[λ]αίνας ἐπίβαις χθόνος
χλι . [.] . [.] . [.]ν συνόδοισί μ᾽ αὔταις
οἴκημι κ[ά]κων ἔκτος ἔχων πόδας,

ὄππαι Λ[εσβί]αδες κριννόμεναι φύαν
πώλεντ᾽ ἐλκεσίπεπλοι, περὶ δὲ βρέμει
ἄχω θεσπεσία γυναίκων
ἴρα[ς ὀ]λολύγας ἐνιαυσίας . . . .[18]

This is a poem of radical loneliness, which Alkaios emphasises with an oxymoron. 'All alone (*oios*) I have set up my household (*eoikesa*),' he says (at verse ten), but this wording would make little sense to a seventh-century BC ear. The verb (*eoikesa*) is made from the noun *oikos*, which denotes the whole relational complex of spaces, objects, kinsmen, servants, animals, rituals and emotions that constitute life within a family within a *polis*. A man all alone cannot constitute an *oikos*.

Alkaios' oxymoronic condition is reinforced by the kind of creatures that surround him. Wolves and women have replaced 'the fathers of my fathers'. The wolf is a conventional symbol of marginality in Greek poetry. The wolf is an outlaw. He lives beyond the boundary of usefully cultivated and inhabited space marked off as the *polis*, in that blank no-man's-land called *to apeiron* ('the unbounded'). Women, in the ancient view, share this territory spiritually and metaphorically in virtue of a 'natural' female affinity for all that is raw, formless and in need of the civilising hand of man. So, for example, in the document cited by Aristotle that goes by the name of 'The Pythagorean Table of Opposites', we find the attributes curving, dark, secret, evil, ever-moving, not self-contained and lacking its own boundaries aligned with 'Female', set over against straight, light, honest, good, stable, self-contained and firmly bounded on the 'Male' side (Aristotle, *Metaphysics*).[19]

I do not imagine that these polarities or their hierarchisation is news to you, now that classical historians and feminists have spent the last ten or fifteen years codifying the various arguments with which ancient Greek thinkers convinced themselves that women belong to a different race than men. But it interests me that the radical otherness of the female is experienced by Alkaios, as also by Ernest Hemingway, in the form of women's voices uttering sounds that men find bad to hear. Why is female sound bad to hear? The sound that Alkaios hears is that of the local Lesbian women who are conducting beauty contests and making the air reverberate with their yelling. These beauty contests of the Lesbian women are known to us from a notice in the Iliadic scholia which indicates they were an annual event performed probably in honour of Hera. Alkaios mentions the beauty contests in order to remark on their prodigious noise levels and, by so doing, draws his poem into a ring composition. The poem begins with the urbane and orderly sound of a herald summoning male citizens to their rational civic business in the Assembly and the Council. The poem ends with an otherworldly echo of women shrieking in the wolfthickets. Moreover, the women are uttering a particular kind of shriek, the *ololyga*. This is a ritual shout peculiar to females.[20] It is a high-pitched piercing cry uttered at certain climactic moments in ritual practice (e.g. at the moment when a victim's throat is slashed during sacrifice) or at climactic moments in real life (e.g. at the birth of a child) and also a common feature of women's festivals. The *ololyga* with its cognate verb *ololyzo* is one of a family of words, including *eleleu* with its cognate verb *elelizo* and *alala* with its cognate verb *alalazo*, probably of Indo-European origin and obviously of onomatopoeic derivation.[21] These words do not signify anything except their own sound. The sound represents a cry of either intense pleasure or intense pain.[22] To utter such cries is a specialised female function. When Alkaios finds himself surrounded by the sound of the *ololyga* he is telling us that he is completely and genuinely out of bounds. No man would make such a sound. No proper civic space would contain it unregulated. The female festivals in which such ritual cries were heard were generally not permitted to be held within the city limits but were relegated to suburban areas like the mountains, the beach or the rooftops of houses, where women could disport themselves without contaminating the ears or civic space of men. To be exposed to such sound is for Alkaios a condition of political nakedness as alarming as that of his archetype Odysseus, who awakens with no clothes on in a thicket on the island of Phaiakia in the sixth book of Homer's

Odyssey, surrounded by the shrieking of women. 'What a hullabaloo of females comes around me!' Odysseus exclaims[23] and goes on to wonder what sort of savages or supernatural beings can be making such a racket. The savages, of course, turn out to be Nausikaa and her girlfriends playing soccer on the riverbank, but what is interesting in this scenario is Odysseus' automatic association of disorderly female sound with wild space, with savagery and the supernatural. Nausikaa and her friends are shortly compared by Homer to the wild girls who roam the mountains in attendance upon Artemis,[24] a goddess herself notorious for the sounds that she makes – if we may judge from her Homeric epithets. Artemis is called *keladeine*, derived from the noun *kelados*, which means a loud roaring noise as of wind or rushing water or the tumult of battle. Artemis is also called *iocheaira*, which is usually etymologised to mean 'she who pours forth arrows' (from *ios* meaning 'arrow'), but could just as well come from the exclamatory sound *io* and mean 'she who pours forth the cry *IO!*'[25]

Greek women of the archaic and classical periods were not encouraged to pour forth unregulated cries of any kind within the civic space of the *polis* or within earshot of men. Indeed masculinity in such a culture defines itself by its different use of sound. Verbal continence is an essential feature of the masculine virtue of *sophrosyne* ('prudence, soundness of mind, moderation, temperance, self-control') that organises most patriarchal thinking on ethical or emotional matters. Woman as a species is frequently said to lack the ordering principle of *sophrosyne*. Freud formulates the double standard succinctly in a remark to a colleague: 'A thinking man is his own legislator and confessor, and obtains his own absolution, but the woman . . . does not have the measure of ethics in herself. She can only act if she keeps within the limits of morality, following what society has established as fitting.'[26] So too, ancient discussions of the virtue of *sophrosyne* demonstrate clearly that, where it is applied to women, this word has a different definition than for men.[27] Female *sophrosyne* is coextensive with female obedience to male direction and rarely means more than chastity. When it does mean more, the allusion is often to sound. A husband exhorting his wife or concubine to *sophrosyne* is likely to mean 'Be quiet!'[28] The Pythagorean heroine Timyche who bit off her tongue rather than say the wrong thing is praised as an exception to the female rule.[29] In general, the women of classical literature are a species given to disorderly and uncontrolled outflows of sound – to shrieking, wailing, sobbing, shrill lament, loud laughter, screams of pain or of pleasure and eruptions of raw emotion in general. As Euripides puts it, 'For it is woman's inborn pleasure always to have her current emotions coming up to her mouth and out through her tongue' (*Andromache*).[30] When a man lets his current emotions come up to his mouth and out through his tongue he is thereby feminised, as Herakles at the end of the *Trachiniai* agonises to find himself, 'sobbing like a girl, whereas before I used to follow my difficult course without a groan but now in pain I am discovered a woman'.[31]

It is a fundamental assumption of these gender stereotypes that a man in his proper condition of *sophrosyne* should be able to dissociate himself from his own emotions and so control their sound. It is a corollary assumption that man's proper civic responsibility towards woman is to control her sound for her insofar as she cannot control it herself. We see a summary moment of such masculine benevolence in Homer's *Odyssey* in Book 22 when the old woman Eurykleia enters the dining hall to find Odysseus caked in blood and surrounded by dead suitors. Eurykleia lifts her head and opens her mouth to utter an *ololyga*. Whereupon Odysseus reaches out a hand and closes her mouth, saying *ou themis*: 'It is not permitted for you to scream just now. Rejoice inwardly . . .'[32]

Closing women's mouths was the object of a complex

array of legislation and convention in preclassical and classical Greece, of which the best documented examples are Solon's sumptuary laws and the core concept is Sophokles' blanket statement 'Silence is the *kosmos* [good order] of women.'[33] The sumptuary laws enacted by Solon in the sixth century BC had as their effect, Plutarch tells us, 'to forbid all the disorderly and barbarous excesses of women in their festivals, processions and funeral rites'.[34] The main responsibility for funeral lament had belonged to women from the earliest Greek times. Already in Homer's *Iliad* we see the female Trojan captives in Achilles' camp compelled to wail over Patroklos.[35] Yet lawgivers of the sixth and fifth centuries like Solon were at pains to restrict these female outpourings to a minimum of sound and emotional display.

The official rhetoric of the lawgivers is instructive. It tends to denounce bad sound as political disease (*nosos*) and speaks of the need to purify civic spaces of such pollution. Sound itself is regarded as the means of purification as well as of pollution. So for example the lawgiver Charondas, who laid down laws for the city of Katana in Sicily, prefaced his legal code with a ceremonial public *katharsis*. This took the form of an incantation meant to cleanse the citizen body of evil ideas or criminal intent and to prepare a civic space for the legal *katharsis* that followed. In his law code, Charondas, like Solon, was concerned to regulate female noise and turned attention to the ritual funeral lament. Laws were passed specifying the location, time, duration, personnel, choreography, musical content and verbal content of the women's funeral lament on the grounds that these 'harsh and barbaric sounds' were a stimulus to 'disorder and licence' (as Plutarch puts it).[36] Female sound was judged to arise in craziness and to generate craziness.

We detect a certain circularity in the reasoning here. If women's public utterance is perpetually enclosed within cultural institutions like the ritual lament, if women are regularly reassigned to the expression of nonrational sounds like the *ololyga* and raw emotion in general, then the so-called 'natural' tendency of the female to shrieking, wailing, weeping, emotional display and oral disorder cannot help but become a self-fulfilling prophecy. But circularity is not the most ingenious thing about this reasoning. We should look a little more closely at the ideology that underlies male abhorrence of female sound. And it becomes important at this point to distinguish sound from language.

For the formal definition of human nature preferred by patriarchal culture is one based on articulation of sound. As

Aristotle says, any animal can make noises to register pleasure or pain. But what differentiates man from beast, and civilization from the wilderness, is the use of rationally articulated speech: *logos*.[37] From such a prescription for humanity follow severe rules for what constitutes human *logos*. When the wife of Alexander Graham Bell, a woman who had been deafened in childhood and knew how to lip-read but not how to talk very well, asked him to teach her sign language, Alexander replied, 'The use of sign language is pernicious. For the only way by which language can be thoroughly mastered is by using it for the communication of thought without translation into any other language.'[38] Alexander Graham Bell's wife, whom he had married the day after he patented the telephone, never did learn sign language. Or other any language.

What is it that is pernicious about sign language? To a husband like Alexander Graham Bell, as to a patriarchal social order like that of classical Greece, there is something disturbing or abnormal about the use of signs to transcribe upon the outside of the body a meaning from inside the body which does not pass through the control point of *logos*, a meaning which is not subject to the mechanism of dissociation that the Greeks called *sophrosyne* or self-control. Sigmund Freud applied the name 'hysteria' to this process of transcription when it occurred in female patients whose tics and neuralgias and convulsions and paralyses and eating disorders and spells of blindness could be read, in his theory, as a direct translation into somatic terms of psychic events within the woman's body.[39] Freud conceived his own therapeutic task as the rechannelling of these hysteric signs into rational discourse.[40] Herodotos tells us of a priestess of Athene in Pedasa who did not use speech to prophesy but would grow a beard whenever she saw misfortune coming upon her community.[41] Herodotos does not register any surprise at the 'somatic compliance' (as Freud would call it) of this woman's prophetic body, nor call her condition pathological. But Herodotos was a practical person, less concerned to discover pathologies in his historical subjects than to congratulate them for putting 'otherness' to cultural use. And the anecdote does give us a strong image of how ancient culture went about constructing the 'otherness' of the female. Woman is that creature who puts the inside on the outside. By projections and leakages of all kinds – somatic, vocal, emotional, sexual – females expose or expend what should be kept in. Females blurt out a direct translation of what should be formulated indirectly. There is a story told about the wife of Pythagoras, that she once uncovered her arm while out of doors and someone commented, 'Nice arm,' to which she responded, 'Not public property!' Plutarch's comment on this story is: 'The arm of a virtuous woman should not be public property, nor her speech neither, and she should as modestly guard against exposing her voice to outsiders as she would guard against stripping off her clothes. For in her voice as she is blabbering away can be read her emotions, her character and her physical condition.'[42] In spite of herself, Plutarch's woman has a voice that acts like a sign language, exposing her inside facts. Ancient physiologists from Aristotle through to the early Roman empire tell us that a man can know from the sound of a woman's voice private data like whether or not she is menstruating, whether or not she has had sexual experience.[43] Although these are useful things to know, they may be bad to hear or make men uncomfortable. What is pernicious about sign language is that it permits a direct continuity between inside and outside. Such continuity is abhorrent to the male nature. The masculine virtue of *sophrosyne* or self-control aims to obstruct this continuity, to dissociate the outside surface of a man from what is going on inside him. Man breaks continuity by interposing *logos* – whose most important censor is the rational articulation sound.

Every sound we make is a bit of autobiography. It has a totally private interior yet its trajectory is public. A piece of inside projected to the outside. The censorship of such projections is a task of patriarchal culture that (as we have seen) divides humanity into two species: those who can censor themselves and those who cannot.

In order to explore some of the implications of this division let us consider how Plutarch depicts the two species in his essay 'On Talkativeness'.

To exemplify the female species in its use of sound Plutarch tells the story of a politician's wife who is tested by her husband. The politician makes up a crazy story and tells it to his wife as a secret early one morning. 'Now keep your mouth closed about this,' he warns her. The wife immediately relates the secret to her maidservant. 'Now keep your mouth closed about this,' she tells the maidservant, who immediately relates it to the whole town and before midmorning the politician himself receives his own story back again. Plutarch concludes this anecdote by saying, 'The husband had taken precautions and protective measures in order to test his wife, as one might test a cracked or leaky vessel by filling it not with oil or wine but with water.'[44] Plutarch pairs this anecdote with a story about masculine speech acts. It is a description of a friend of Solon's named Anacharsis:

> Anacharsis, who had dined with Solon and was resting after dinner, was seen pressing his left hand on his sexual parts and his right hand on his mouth: for he believed that the tongue requires a more powerful restraint. And he was right. It would not be easy to count as many men lost through incontinence in amorous pleasures as cities and empires ruined through revelation of a secret.[45]

In assessing the implications of the gendering of sound for a society like that of the ancient Greeks, we have to take seriously the connection Plutarch makes between verbal and sexual continence, between mouth and genitals. Because that connection turns out to be a very different matter for men than for women. The masculine virtue of self-censorship with which Anacharsis responds to impulses from inside himself is shown to be simply unavailable to the female nature. Plutarch reminds us a little later in the essay that perfect *sophrosyne* is an attribute of the god Apollo, whose epithet Loxias means that he is a god of few words and concise expression, not one who runs off at the mouth.[46] Now when a woman runs off at the mouth there is far more at stake than waste of words: the image of the leaky water jar with which Plutarch concludes his first anecdote is one of the commonest figures in ancient literature for the representation of female sexuality.

The forms and contexts of this representation (the leaky jar of female sexuality) have been studied at length by other scholars including me,[47] so let us pass directly to the heart, or rather the mouth, of the matter. It is an axiom of ancient Greek and Roman medical theory and anatomical discussion that a woman has two mouths.[48] The orifice through which vocal activity takes place and the orifice through which sexual activity takes place are both denoted by the word *stoma* in Greek (*os* in Latin) with the addition of adverbs *ano* or *kato* to differentiate upper mouth from lower mouth. Both the vocal and the genital mouth are connected to the body by a neck (*auchen* in Greek, *cervix* in Latin). Both mouths provide access to a hollow cavity which is guarded by lips that are best kept closed. The ancient medical writers apply not only homologous terms but also parallel medications to upper and lower mouths in certain cases of uterine malfunction. They note with interest, as do many poets and scholiasts, symptoms of physiological response between upper and lower mouth, for example that an excess or blockage of blood in the uterus will evidence itself as strangulation or loss of voice,[49] that too much vocal exercise results in loss of menses,[50] that defloration causes a woman's neck to enlarge and her voice to deepen.[51]

'With a high pure voice because she has not yet been acted upon by the bull' is how Aiskhylos describes his Iphigeneia (*Agamemnon*).[52] The changed voice and enlarged throat of the sexually initiated female are an upward projection of irrevocable changes at the lower mouth. Once a woman's sexual life begins, the lips of the uterus are never completely closed again – except on one occasion, as the medical writers explain: in his treatise on gynaecology Soranos describes the sensations that a woman experiences during fruitful sexual intercourse. At the moment of conception, the Hellenistic doctor Soranos alleges, the woman has a shivering sensation and the perception that the mouth of her uterus closes upon the seed.[53] This closed mouth, and the good silence of conception that it protects and signifies, provides the model of decorum for the upper mouth as well. Sophokles' frequently cited dictum, 'Silence is the *kosmos* of women', has its medical analogue in women's amulets from antiquity which picture a uterus equipped with a lock at the mouth.

When it is not locked the mouth may gape open and let out unspeakable things. Greek myth, literature and cult show traces of cultural anxiety about such female ejaculation. For example, there is the story of Medusa who, when her head was cut off by Perseus, gave birth to a son and a flying horse through her neck.[54] Or again that restless and loquacious nymph Echo, surely the most mobile female in Greek myth. When Sophokles calls her 'the girl with no door on her mouth', we might wonder which mouth he means. Especially since Greek legend marries Echo off in the end to the god Pan whose name implies her conjugal union with every living thing.

We should also give some consideration to that bizarre and variously explained religious practice called *aischrologia*. *Aischrologia* means, 'saying ugly things'. Certain women's festivals included an interval in which women shouted abusive remarks or obscenities or dirty jokes at one another. Historians of religion classify these rituals of bad sound either as some Frazerian species of fertility magic or as a type of coarse but cheering buffoonery in which (as Walter Burkert says) 'antagonism between the sexes is played up and finds release'.[55] But the fact remains that in general men were not welcome at these rituals and Greek legend contains more than a few cautionary tales of men castrated, dismembered or killed when they blundered into them.[56] These stories suggest a backlog of sexual anger behind the bland face of religious buffoonery. Ancient society was happy to have women drain off such unpleasant tendencies and raw emotion into a leakproof ritual container. The strategy involved here is a kathartic one, based on a sort of psychological division of labour between the sexes, such as (pseudo)Demosthenes mentions in a reference to the Athenian ritual called Choes. The ceremony of Choes took place on the second day of the Dionysian festival of Anthesteria.[57] It featured a competition between celebrants to drain an oversized jug of wine and concluded with a symbolic (or perhaps not) act of sexual union between the god Dionysos and a representative woman of the community. It is this person to whom Demosthenes refers, saying: 'She is the woman who discharges the unspeakable things on behalf of the city.'[58]

Let us dwell for a moment on this ancient female task of discharging unspeakable things on behalf of the city, and on the structures that the city sets up to contain such speech.

A ritual structure like the *aischrologia* raises some difficult questions of definition. For it collapses into a single kathartic activity two different aspects of sound production. We have noticed this combinatory tactic already throughout most of the ancient and some of the modern discussions of voice: female sound is bad to hear both because the quality of a woman's voice is objectionable and because woman uses her voice to say what should not be said. When these two aspects are blurred together, some important questions about the distinction between essential and constructed characteristics of human nature recede into circularity. Nowadays, sex difference in language is a topic of diverse research and unresolved debate. The sounds made by women are said to have different inflectional patterns, different ranges of intonation, different syntactic preferences, different semantic fields, different diction, different narrative textures, different behavioural accoutrements, different contextual pressures than the sounds that men make.[59] Tantalising vestiges of ancient evidence for such difference may be read from, for example, passing references in Aristophanes to a 'woman's language', that a man can learn or imitate if he wants to (*Thesmophoriazousai*),[60] or from the conspicuously onomatopoeic construction of female cries like *ololuga* and female names like Gorgo, Baubo, Echo, Syrinx, Eileithyia.[61] But in general, no clear account of the ancient facts can be extracted from strategically blurred notions like the homology of female mouth and female genitals, or tactically blurred activities like the ritual of the *aischrologia*. What does emerge is a consistent paradigm of response to otherness of voice. It is a paradigm that forms itself as *katharsis*.

As such, the ancient Greek ritual of *aischrologia* bears

some resemblance to the procedure developed by Sigmund Freud and his colleague Josef Breuer for treatment of hysterical women. In *Studies on Hysteria* (1895), Freud and Breuer use the term 'katharsis' and also the term 'talking cure' of this revolutionary therapy. In Freud's theory the hysterical patients are women who have bad memories or ugly emotions trapped inside them like a pollution. Freud and Breuer find themselves able to drain off this pollution by inducing the women under hypnosis to speak unspeakable things. Hypnotised women produce some remarkable sounds. One of the case studies described by Freud can at first only clack like a hen; another insists on speaking English although she is Viennese; another uses what Freud calls 'paraphrastic jargon'.[62] But all are eventually channelled by the psychoanalyst into connected narrative and rational exegesis of their hysteric symptoms. Whereupon, both Freud and Breuer claim, the symptoms disappear – cleansed by this simple kathartic ritual of draining off the bad sound of unspeakable things.

Here is how Josef Breuer describes his interaction with the patient who goes by the pseudonym Anna O:

> ... I used to visit her in the evening, when I knew I should find her in her hypnosis, and then I relieved her of the whole stock of imaginative products which she had accumulated since my last visit. It

> was essential that this should be effected completely if good results were to follow. When this was done she became perfectly calm, and next day she would be agreeable, easy to manage, industrious and even cheerful . . . She aptly described this procedure as a 'talking cure', while she referred to it jokingly as 'chimney sweeping'.[63]

Whether we call it chimney sweeping or *aischrologia* or ritual funeral lament or a hullabaloo of females or having a laugh like a beefsteak, the same paradigm of response is obvious. As if the entire female gender were a kind of collective bad memory of unspeakable things, patriarchal order, like a well-intentioned psychoanalyst, seems to conceive of its therapeutic responsibility as the channelling of bad sound into politically appropriate containers. Both the upper and the lower female mouth apparently stand in need of such controlling action. Freud mentions shyly in a footnote to *Case Studies on Hysteria* that Josef Breuer had to suspend his analytic relationship with Anna O. because 'she suddenly made manifest to Breuer the presence of a strongly unanalysed positive transference of an unmistakably sexual nature'.[64] Not until 1932 did Freud reveal (in a letter to a colleague)[65] what really happened between Breuer and Anna O. It was on the evening of his last interview with her that Breuer entered Anna's apartment to find her on the floor contorted by abdominal pain. When he asked her what was wrong she answered that she was about to give birth to his child. It was this 'untoward event', as Freud calls it, that caused Breuer to hold back the publication of *Case Studies on Hysteria* from 1881 to 1895 and led him ultimately to abandon collaborating with Freud. Even the talking cure must fall silent when both female mouths try to speak at the same time.

It is confusing and embarrassing to have two mouths. Genuine *kakophony* is the sound produced by them. Let us consider one more example from antiquity of female *kakophony* at its most confusing and embarrassing. There is a group of terracotta statues recovered from Asia Minor and dated to the fourth century BC which depict the female body in an alarmingly short-circuited form.[66] Each of these statues is a woman who consists of almost nothing but her two mouths. The two mouths are welded together into an inarticulate body mass which excludes other anatomical function. Moreover the position of the two mouths is reversed. The upper mouth for talking is placed at the bottom of the statue's belly. The lower or genital mouth gapes open on top of the head. Iconographers identify this monster with the old woman named Baubo[67] who figures in Greek legend as an allomorph of the old woman Iambe (in the Demeter myth) and is a sort of patron saint of the ritual of the *aischrologia*. Baubo's name has a double significance; according to the Liddell, Scott, Jones Ancient Greek Lexicon the noun *baubo* is used as a synonym for *koilia* (which denotes the female uterus) but as a piece of sound it derives from *baubau*, the onomatopoeic Greek word for a dog's bark.[68] The mythic action of Baubo is also significantly double. Like the old woman Iambe, Baubo is credited in legend with the twofold gesture of pulling up her clothes to reveal her genitalia and also shouting out obscene language or jokes. The shouting of Baubo provides one aetiology for the ritual of the *aischrologia*; her action of genital exposure may also have come over into cult as a ritual action called the *anasyrma* (the 'pulling up' of clothing).[69] If so, we may understand this action as a kind of visual or gestural noise, projected outwards upon circumstances to change or deflect them, in the manner of an apotropaic utterance. So Plutarch describes the use of the *anasyrma* gesture by women in besieged cities: in order to repel the enemy they stand on the city wall and pull up their clothing to expose unspeakable things.[70] Plutarch praises this action of female self-exposure as an instance of virtue in its context. But woman's allegedly definitive tendency to put the inside on the outside could provoke quite another reaction. The Baubo statues are strong evidence of that reaction. This Baubo presents us with one simple chaotic diagram of an outrageously manipulable female identity. The doubling and interchangeability of mouth engenders a creature in whom sex is cancelled out by sound and sound is cancelled out by sex. This seems a perfect answer to all the questions raised and dangers posed by the confusing and embarrassing continuity of female nature. Baubo's mouths appropriate each other.

Cultural historians disagree on the meaning of these statues. They have no certain information on the gender or intention or state of mind of the people who made them. We can only guess at their purpose as objects or their mood as works of art. Personally I find them as ugly and confusing and almost funny as *Playboy* magazine in its current predilection for placing centrefold photographs of naked women side by side with long, intensely empathetic articles about high-profile feminists. This is more than an oxymoron. There is a death of meaning in the collocation of such falsehoods – each of them, the centrefold naked woman and the feminist, a social construct purchased and marketed by *Playboy* magazine to facilitate that fantasy of masculine virtue that the ancient Greeks called *sophrosyne* and Freud renamed repression.

In considering the question 'How do our presumptions about gender affect the way we hear sounds?' I have cast my net rather wide and have mingled evidence from different periods of time and different forms of cultural expression – in a way that reviewers of my work like to dismiss as ethnographic naïveté. I think there is a place for naïveté in ethnography, at the very least as an irritant. Sometimes when I am reading a Greek text I force myself to look up all the words in the dictionary, even the ones I think I know. It is surprising what you learn that way. Some of the words turn out to sound quite different than you thought. Sometimes the way they sound can make you ask questions you wouldn't otherwise ask. Lately I have begun to question the Greek word *sophrosyne*. I wonder about this concept of self-control and whether it really is, as the Greeks believed, an answer to most questions of human goodness and dilemmas of civility. I wonder if there might not be another idea of human order than repression, another notion of human virtue than self-control, another kind of human self than one based on dissociation of inside and outside. Or indeed, another human essence than self.

Endnotes

1 *Physiognomics*, 807a.

2 *Physiognomios*, 813a. On *kinaidos* see Aiskhines 1.131 and 2.99; Dover (1975), 17, 75; M.W. Gleason (1990), 401; I am indebted to Maud Gleason also for allowing me to preview a chapter ('The Role of the Voice in the Maintenance of Gender Boundaries') of her book on self-presentation in the Second Sophistic, *Making Men: Sophists and Self-Presentation in Ancient Rome*.

3 Aristophanes, *Ekklesiazousai*, 113-114.

4 Aristotle, *On the Generation of Animals*, 787b-788.

5 Oribasios, 6; Gleason (1994), 12.

6 A. Raphael, *The Observer*, October 7, 1979.

7 S. Rogers in S. Ardener (1981), 59.

8 T. Howe (1954), 209; J.-P. Vernant (1991), 117.

9 *Eumenides*, 117, 131.

10 *Odyssey*, 4.275.

11 Aiskhylos, *Agamemnon*, 1213-14.

12 *Homeric Hymn to Aphrodite*, 18-20.

13 *Iliad*, 14.216.

14 On Iambe see M. Olender (1990), 85-90 and references.

15 *Philoktetes*, 188.

16 M. D. Luhan (1935), 324.

17 E. Hemingway (1964), 118.

18 fr. 130 Lobel.

19 Aristotle, *Metaphysics*, 986a22.

20 S. Eitrem (1919). III, 44-53 assembles the pertinent texts.

21 E. Boisacq (1907), 698.

22 L. Gernet (1983), 248 and n. 8.

23 *Od.* 9. 105-6.

24 *Od.* 9. 105-6.

25 So Gernet (1983), 249-250 following Ehrlich (1910), 48.

26 Letter to E. Silberstein cited by Grosskurth (1980), 889.

27 H. North (1966), see especially 1, 22, 37, 59, 206.

28 E.g. Sophokles, *Ajax,* 586.

29 Iamblichos, *Life of Pythagoras,* 31, 194.

30 *Andromache,* 94-95.

31 1070-5.

32 *Od.* 22. 405-6.

33 Cited by Aristotle, *Politics,* 1, 1260a30.

34 Life of Solon, 21 = *Moralia,* 65b.

35 18.339.

36 *Ibid.,* 12.5 and 21.4. I learn from Marilyn Katz that there is serious contemporary debate about Jewish women praying aloud (i.e., reading from the Torah) at the Western Wall in Jerusalem: 'The principal objection that I have heard has to do with the men's enforced exposure to *kol ishah* (female voice) from which they are normally expected to be protected, for a vast array of reasons articulated by rabbis in the Talmud and elsewhere, including sexual temptation.'

37 *Politics,* 1253a.

38 This anecdote formed part of a lecture A.G.B. delivered to the Social Science Association, Boston, December 1871.

39 S. Freud and J. Breuer (1965).

40 'We found that each individual hysterical symptom immediately and permanently disappeared when we had succeeded

in bringing clearly to light the memory of the event by which it was provoked and . . . when the patient had described that event in the greatest possible detail and had put the affect into words.' Freud goes on to say that the psycho-therapeutic method works 'by allowing strangulated affect to find a way out through speech' (Ibid., 6, 253).

41 1.75.

42 *Life of Pythagoras, 7 = Moralia,* 142d; Gleason, 65.

43 Aristotle, *History of Animals,* 581a31-b5; Suidas *s.v. Diagnomon;* Gleason 53; A. Hanson and I. Armstrong (1986), 97-100; A. Hanson (1990), 328-329 and references.

44 *On Talkativeness. 7 = Moralia,* 507b-d.

45 *Ibid., 7 = Moralia,* 505a.

46 *Ibid., 17 = Moralia,* 511b6-10.

47 The logic of the representation has obviously to do with male observation of the mysteriously unfailing moistures of female physiology and also with a prevailing ancient medical conception of the female uterus as an upside down jar. See Carson (1990); A. Hanson (1990), 325-327; G. Sissa (1990), 125-157.

48 Hippokrates, *Diseases of Women,* 2.137, 8.310.5 (Littré); Galen, *On the Usefulness of Parts,* 15.3; Hanson (1990), 321-329; Olender (1990), 104-105; Sissa (1990), 5, 53-66, 70, 166-68.

49 Galen, *On Generation,* 15.2-3; Hanson (1990), 328.

50 Soranos, *Gynaikeia;* 1.4.22; Gleason, 122.

51 Aiskhylos, *Agamemnon,* 244; Hanson (1990), 329-332; Hanson and Armstrong (1986).

52 *Agamemnon,* 244.

53 Soranos, *Gynaikeia,* 1.44; *Corpus Medicorum Graecorum,* 4.3.1.9

Illberg: Hanson (1990), 315, 321-322.

54 Hesiod, *Theogony,* 280-281; Wasson et al. (1978), 120.

55 'The Greek evidence points most conspicuously to the absurdity and buffoonery of the whole affair: there is a conscious descent to the lower classes and the lower parts of the anatomy . . .' W. Burkert (1985).

56 Euripides, *Bakkhai;* M. Detienne and J.-P. Vernant (1979), 184-186; F. Zeitlin (1982), 146-153.

57 On the Anthesteria see Parke (1977), 107-113; Burkert (1985), 239.

58 59.73.

59 See, for example, Adler (1978); Cixous (1981); Gatens (1991), especially 6-84; Irigaray (1990); Kramarae (1981); Lakoff (1975); Sapir (1949); Spender (1985).

60 Aristophanes, *Thesmophoriazousai,* 192, 267.

61 See also Zeitlin (1985) on the feminisation of the male in Greek tragedy.

62 Freud and Breuer (1966), 5-17, 29.

63 *Ibid.,* 30.

64 *Ibid.,* 40 n. 1.

65 Gay (1988), 67.

66 Olender (1990) and plates.

67 H. Diels made the identification (1907); on Baubo see further A.N. Athanassakis (1976); Burkert (1985), 368; Devereux (1983): Graf (1974), 169, 171; Lobeck (1829); Olender (1990).

68 Olender suggests another explanation, associated with nursing an infant: (1990), 97-99 and references.

69 Graf (1974), 169, 195; Olender (1990), 93-95.

70 *On the Virtue of Women,* 5.9 = *Moralia,* 532f.